My name's not
Gordon Trafficwarden,
My name's not
Mary Secretary,
My name's not
Hector Rentcollector,
My name's not
Lena Windowcleaner,
My name's not
Sacha Haberdasher,
My name is
Becky Hamilton
And this book belongs to ME!

Also available by Colin West

Not To Be Taken Seriously
The Land of Utter Nonsense

A STEP IN THE WRONG DIRECTION

Poems and Pictures by Colin West

Beaver Books

A Beaver Book

Published by Arrow Books Limited
17-21 Conway Street, London W1P 6JD

An imprint of the Hutchinson Publishing Group

London Melbourne Sydney Auckland
Johannesburg and agencies throughout
the world

First published in this edition by Hutchinson 1984
Beaver edition 1985
First published as two volumes: *Out of the Blue
From Nowhere* 1976 and *Back to Front and Back
Again* 1980 by Dobson Books Ltd, Durham

Printed and bound in Great Britain by
Anchor Brendon Limited, Tiptree, Essex

ISBN 0 09 940600 4

CONTENTS

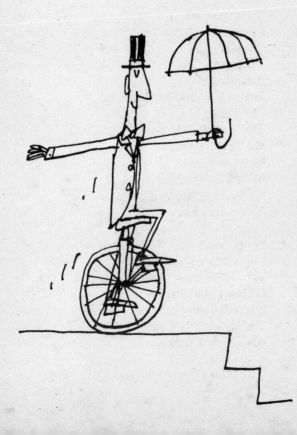

A Wisp of a Wasp

I'm a wisp of a wasp with a worry,
I'm hiding somewhere in Surrey,
I've just bit upon
The fat sit upon
Of the King – so I left in a hurry!

Eat Your Food Up, Artie

Artie, Artie, eat your food up,
Eat your food up, Artie;
You look the sort that never has
A meal that's good and hearty.

Artie, Artie, eat your food up,
Eat your tripe and onions;
For if you don't, your feet will have
A nasty bout of bunions.

Artie, Artie, eat your food up,
Eat your beef and carrots;
Unless you want to grow a beak
And feathers like a parrot's.

Artie, Artie, eat your food up,
Artie I'm not joking.
(So Artie ate an artichoke,
Now look at Artie choking.)

Artie, Artie, cough your food up,
Cough your food up, Artie;
I'll eat my words and we shall have
Just jelly at your party!

The Gobblegulp

The Gobblegulp is most uncouth,
In his mouth is just one tooth,
He gobbles food and gulps Ribena
Like a living vacuum cleaner.
He has a great big bulging belly
That wobbles when he walks like jelly,
But what I like about him least
Is that he is a noisy beast,
For when he eats an apple crumble,
His tummy starts to roll and rumble;
I often hear a noise and wonder,
'Was that a Gobblegulp – or thunder?'

Ethel Read a Book

Ethel read, Ethel read,
Ethel read a book.
Ethel read a book in bed,
She read a book on Ethelred.
The book that Ethel read in bed,
(The book on Ethelred) was red.
The book was red that Ethel read,
In bed on Ethelred.

She Likes to Swim Beneath the Sea

She likes to swim beneath the sea
And wear her rubber flippers,
She likes to dance outrageously
And wake up all the kippers.

The Saddest Spook

The saddest spook there ever was,
Is melancholious because
He can't so much as raise a sneer,
Or laugh a laugh that's vaguely queer.

He hasn't learned to walk through walls,
And dares not answer wolfish calls,
And when big ghosts are rude and coarse,
And shout at him: 'Your fangs are false,'

He smiles at them, just like a fool,
But wishes they'd pick on a ghoul
Who's heavyweight and not just bantam,
Why pick on a little phantom?

Nasty Norman Nosher

The horriblest boy I know of,
The horriblest boy by far,
(The sort I'd gladly strangle
If permitted to by law)
Is Nasty Norman Nosher,
A most unwholesome lout,
Who yells when others whisper,
And laughs when others shout.

I hate his boots and braces,
I hate his socks and toes,
I hate his plastic spider joke,
I hate his runny nose;

I hate the way he loafs around,
The lazy little lout,
I hate the way his bubblegum
Is always dropping out.

I hate him more than anyone,
I hate him more than Keith,
I even hate the one-inch gap
Between his two front teeth.
I hate his dirty fingernails,
I hate him from his head,
Right down to his two smelly feet,
I'd rather see him dead!

Hither and Thither

Hither and thither,
She plays on the zither,
Her music is ever so mellow;
But don't stop and dither,
Just look who is with her –
Her husband who's playing the cello.

He scratches and screeches,
The high notes he reaches
Sound more like a cat being sat on;
Conductors throw peaches
When passing, and each is
Soon seen to be breaking his baton.

Both crotchet and quaver
Seem somehow to savour
A key neither major nor minor,
And if I were braver,
I'd ask him a favour,
'Why *don't* you please practise in China?'

Lanky Lee
and Lindy Lou

Said Lanky Lee
To Lindy Lou,
'Please let me run
Away with you!'
But Lou replied
With frustration:
'You've got no
Imagination,
For that is all,
Dear Lanky Lee,
That ever runs
Away with *me*!'

My Uncle is a Baronet

My uncle is a baronet,
He sleeps beside the hearth,
And likes to play the clarinet
Whilst sitting in the bath.

Marmaduke the Noisy Knight

In Arthur's reign or thereabouts,
When fellows drank from flagons,
A knight who knew the whereabouts
Of unicorns or dragons
Was very likely to impress
A dozen damsels in distress.

But one poor knight named Marmaduke,
Who'd never bravely battled,
Could not so much as harm a duke,
Because his armour rattled.
And when he moved, he couldn't hide
The noises coming from inside.

He never dared, like Lancelot,
Queen Guinevere to flatter,
For never could he dance a lot,
As he was bound to clatter.

And Marmaduke was most provoked
When ladies laughed and jesters joked.

At last he told a farmer off
Who ridiculed his rattle,
And then he tore his armour off
In front of all the cattle,
And as he threw it to the ground,
It gave one final clanging sound.

He then ran off, I wonder where
On earth he might have gone to?
He only had his underwear
And helmet to hang onto.
He must have made a sorry sight,
Poor Marmaduke the Noisy Knight.

Trevor is Ever so

Trevor is ever so clever,
Trevor is ever so clean,
Trevor is welcome wherever
Trevor is heard or is seen.

Trevor is ever so handsome,
Trevor is ever so nice,
Trevor is worth any ransom,
Trevor is worth any price.

Trevor is ever so charming,
Trevor is ever so sweet,
Trevor is never alarming,
Trevor is truly a treat.

Trevor is ever so youthful,
Trevor is ever so bright,
Trevor is ever so truthful,
Trevor is very polite.

Trevor is ever so modest,
Trevor, oh how do I know?
Trevor, the thing I find oddest:
Trevor *alone* told me so!

The Prize Pumpkin

They seized it, they squeezed it,
They gave it funny looks,
They teased it, they eased it,
They looked it up in books.
They tethered it, they weathered it,
They even tarred and feathered it,
And when they could, they measured it,
(It came to seven foot).

They gave it a prod,
They gave it a poke,
They sang it a song,
They told it a joke.

They ran to it, they walked to it,
They then began to talk to it.
They lathered it (they rathered it
Was clean as it could be).
They smothered it, they mothered it,
They fathered and they brothered it,
They watered it, they daughtered it,
And sat it on their knee.

They gave it a slap,
They gave it a punch,
They cut it in bits
And had it for lunch!

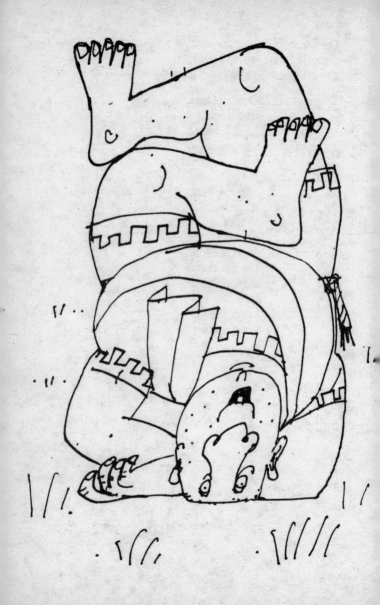

O That Ogre!

O that Ogre,
In a toga,
Doing yoga
On my lawn!
What a prancer,
What a stancer,
Fattest dancer
Ever born!
Watch him tumble,
Feel him fumble,
Hear him mumble
On till dawn:
'I'm an Ogre
In a toga,
Doing yoga
On your lawn!'

The Wizard and the Lizard

Once a wizard in a blizzard
Caught a lizard down a well.
First he took it, then he shook it,
Did he cook it? Time will tell.

How he stuttered as he muttered,
Till he spluttered out a spell.
Then, hey presto! Full of zest-o.
Have you guessed? O do not yell!

It was tragic that his magic
Word *Kadagic* wasn't right;
For the lizard in the blizzard
Gave the wizard quite a fright.

It grew larger than a Rajah,
With a barge, a butt, a bite,
First it fizzled, till it grizzled,
Then it sizzled out of sight.

In Monster Town

The rain came down in Monster Town
And trickled down the drain;
Two Monsters sat on Platform One
And waited for a train.

Said Monster Boy to Monster Girl,
'Your feet I so admire,
Your Monster Toes, they seem to set
My Monster Nose on fire.

'And under your umbrella here,
You make me feel so snug,
Pray take me to your Monster Heart,
Let's have a Monster Hug!'

And so they squeezed each other tight,
The way that Monsters do,
Till all their Monster Teeth were black,
And all their bones were blue.

Then Monster Girl to Monster Boy
Cried, 'Hark! Here comes the train.'
As rain came down in Monster Town
And trickled down the drain.

Parsons, Priests and Country Vicars

Parsons, priests and country vicars
Love the food of city slickers,
They go to cafés with their vergers
For crinkle chips and cheesyburgers;
They shake on ketchup, spread on mustard,
And wash it down with prunes and custard!

What do Teachers Dream of?

What do teachers dream of,
In mountains and in lowlands?
They dream of exclamation marks,
Full stops and semi-colons!

I Saw Your Hornrimmed Glasses

I saw your hornrimmed glasses,
I recognized your nose;
You're not the same, you've dyed your hair,
You've had a change of clothes.

Now me, I've got this molar,
It's causing me great pain,
So can't you drill a hole in it,
Until we meet again?

What's that, you're not my dentist,
You're not my Mister Glue?
You spend your life in Barnstaple,
You've never been to Looe?

But you've got his ears and habits.
That gait can't be your own;
I can't believe that you're not he,
I *won't* leave you alone!

Deborah, Deborah

Deborah, Deborah, Deborah is it
Possible for you to visit
Far-off lands that are exquisite,
And though I wouldn't *force* you,
I hear the Outer Hebrides
Are beautiful, so Deborah please,
Ride off upon my zebra, he's
Just waiting for a horseshoe!

Rumbletumtoo

O what a morning, let's leap out of bed,
I'm glad that I'm living, I'm glad I'm not dead,
I'm happy and humble, and how about you,
Aren't you glad to be living in Rumbletumtoo?

In Rumbletumtoo we sizzle and spark,
We sleep with the owl and we rise with the lark,
We're yokels who yodel, we know what to do,
We're glad to be living in Rumbletumtoo!

In Rumbletumtoo we whistle a tune,
To bring out the sun and to banish the moon,
O isn't it gorgeous, O isn't it grand,
That we are not living in Snickerboxland?

In Snickerboxland they grumble and grouse,
They work like the beaver and eat like the mouse,
Their heads are hung heavy, they wish through and
    through,
That they could be living in Rumbletumtoo!

Crocodile or Alligator?

Crocodile or alligator,
Who is who on the equator?
Which one ate up Auntie Norah,
Famous tropical explorer?

Cool she was and calm she kept, I'll
Bet you that repulsive reptile
Had a hard job as he ate her,
Crocodile *or* alligator.

Norah, sister of my mother,
Couldn't tell one from the other;
Had she only read this fable,
Maybe she'd have then been able.

Crocodiles, with jaws shut tightly,
Show their teeth off impolitely;
But alligators aren't so rude,
And seldom let their teeth protrude.

Whether former, whether latter,
To Aunt Norah doesn't matter;
She's at rest inside his tummy,
What a dinner, yummy, yummy!

If a Man

If a man is never reckless,
If a man is not uncouth,
If a man is never ruthless,
Is he reck and couth and ruth?

Putting the Shot

Tomorrow I may put the shot,
Or on the other hand, may not;
For yesterday I put the shot,
But where I put it, I forgot.

Puddletown

Puddletown is far from here
(Moles have mountains, walls have ears,
Milk is spilt and full of tears)
O take me back to Puddle!

Puddletown is miles from Dover
(People call their kittens Rover,
Some are mauve, the rest are mauver)
O I must go to Puddle!

Puddletown is way down north
(Camels lisp and say: 'Of courth,
I won that rathe by coming fourth')
O let me go to Puddle!

In One Ear and Out the Other

When Miss Tibbs talks
To my dear brother,
It goes in one ear
And out the other;
And when she shouts,
He seldom hears,
The words just whistle
Through his ears.

His ears are big,
(You must've seen 'em)
But he's got nothing
In between 'em.
The truth, Miss Tibbs,
Is hard to face:
His head is full
Of empty space.

The Sloojee

The Sloojee strikes on nights like this,
When everything is still,
It strikes you if you snore too much,
And makes you feel quite ill.

It makes you cry, it makes you weep,
It makes you mutter in your sleep,
It makes you frown, it makes you fidget,
It makes you wish you were a midget.

It makes you wince, it makes you twice,
It makes your kneecaps turn to ice,
It makes you moan, it makes you wail,
It makes you chew your fingernails.

It makes you scream, it makes you shriek,
It makes you itchy for a week,
It makes you shake, it makes you shiver,
It makes you grateful for your liver.

It makes you spit, it makes you shout,
It makes your teeth and hair fall out,
It makes you twitch, it makes you tremble,
It makes your hip joint reassemble.

The Sloojee strikes, and having struck,
The Sloojee slobbers on,
For when you cease to snore out loud,
It knows its job is done.

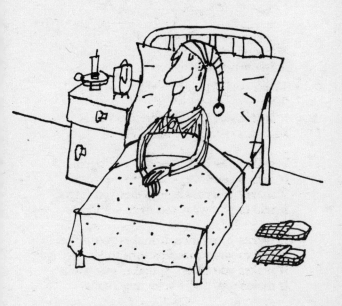

The Song of Silas Bone

The meanest man I've ever known,
Without a doubt is Silas Bone.
He keeps his money in a box
Secured by combination locks.
Some people say, but can't be sure,
He's got a thousand pounds or more.

He rides to town upon his bike
On almost every Friday night,
When moons are high and shops are shut,
And when he feels so full of luck,
That no one ever dares to mock
The song he sings at two o'clock:

'My name is Mister Silas Bone,
The kindest man you've ever known,
I often gamble, often spend,
I often give and often lend,
Some people say, they can but guess,
I've only got a pound or less!'

She Put Her Hair in Curlers

She put her hair in curlers,
She tied it up with bows,
She rode a horse on rollerskates,
A ball upon her nose.

King
Solomon

King
Solomon
was
seldom
sad
when
climbing
up
a
column,
but
when
he
started
sliding
down,
King
Solomon
was
solemn!

Ask a Silly Question

Tell me how in the deep
Does the whale go to sleep,
How does he rest his poor blubber?

He lays down his head
Upon the sea bed,
And snores just like a landlubber!

Tell me why in the sky
Can an ostrich not fly,
Why can't he fly like an eagle?

Because he once heard
From some funny bird
That flying is highly illegal!

Tell me where on the earth
Does the monkey find mirth,
Where does he go to find laughter?

He climbs up a tree
To watch you and me,
Then happily lives ever after!

My Sister is Missing

Harriet, Harriet, jump on your chariot,
My sister is missing, poor Janet!
And Michael, O Michael, go pedal your cycle,
And search every part of the planet.

My sister, my sister, since breakfast I've missed her,
I'll never grow used to the silence;
So Cecil, O Cecil, I'm glad you can wrestle,
For Janet is prone to use violence.

With Doris and Maurice and Horace and Boris
We'll follow the points of the compass,
And if we should find her, we'll creep up behind
    her,
But quietly, for Janet might thump us.

We'll hold her and scold her until we have told her
That running away isn't funny;
But if she says sorry, we'll hire a big lorry,
And drive off to somewhere that's sunny.

We'll wander and ponder in fields over yonder,
But wait! What's that dot in the distance?
It looks like a figure, it's getting much bigger,
It's shouting at all my assistants.

O Janet, my Janet, it can't be, or can it?
My sister is no longer missing!
Hooray! We have found her, let's gather around
    her,
Let's start all the hugging and kissing!

A Penguin's Life

A penguin's life is cold and wet
And always in a muddle,
A penguin's feet are wet and damp
And often in a puddle.

O how ironic! O how absurd!
A penguin cannot fly about
Like any other bird.
O how monotonous,
I'd so much like to be
A big fat hippopotamus
Upon the rolling sea!

A penguin's nose is frozen stiff
And feels just like an icicle,
A penguin has to be content
To live without a bicycle.

O how ironic! O how absurd!
That I'm not supersonic
Like any other bird.
O the frustration,
I'd so much like to hear
The trains at Tooting Station
And the trams at Belvedere!

Euripides

Euripides, Euripodoze,
You always rip your Sunday clothes.
Euripodoze, Euripides,
You always rip them at the knees.

King Canute Cannot

King Canute cannot k-nit,
K-nit Canute cannot;
King Canute cannot k-nit,
King Canute cannot!

I Sometimes Wonder Whether

I sometimes wonder whether
Dear Old Mother Nature ever
Admits she makes a few mistakes,
Such as the porcupine;
And then I start to wonder
About each and every blunder,
And what I'd do to change the world,
If only it were mine.

It seems to me the puma
Doesn't have a sense of humour,
I've never seen a puma try
To make hyenas laugh;
And what about the llama,
Can his life be full of drama,
Or does he wish, as I suspect,
That he were a giraffe?

And then there are those creatures
With the funniest of features,
The mouse or moose or grouse or goose,
To mention but a few;
And bears like the koala,
I'd send to a beauty parlour,
And crocodiles and crabs, I think,
Could also join the queue!

The Darkest and Dingiest Dungeon

Down in the darkest and dingiest dungeon,
Far from the tiniest twinkle of stars,
Far from the whiff of a wonderful luncheon,
Far from the murmur of motoring cars,
Far from the habits of rabbits and weasels,
Far from the merits of ferrets and stoats,
Far from the danger of mumps or of measles,
Far from the fashions of fabulous coats,
Far from the turn of a screw in a socket,
Far from the fresh frozen food in the fridge,
Far from the fluff in my dufflecoat pocket,
Far from the bite of a mischievous midge,
Far from the hole in my humble umbrella,
Far from my hat as it hangs in the hall,
I sit here alone with myself in the cellar,
I *do* so like getting away from it all!

O How I Hate the Poet!

The purpose of a porpoise,
Or a turtle or a tortoise,
Or a salamander well I understand.
The reason for a rumpus,
Or a camel or a compass,
Or a saxophone is plain to any man.

The meaning of a mangle,
Or a congruent triangle,
Or a hemisphere is very clear to see,
But one thing I must mention,
Quite beyond my comprehension,
Is the problem that the poet poses me.
A poet spends his hours
Sat in sofas sniffing flowers,
And writing rhymes as silly as can be.
Just watch him with his poodles,
I would give a hundred roubles
To someone who could explain his use to me.

Where Raindrops Plop

Where raindrops plop in muddy streams,
And thunder shakes the trees,
Where pigs who've played in football teams
Go home in twos and threes;
Where harpists pluck at mournful strings,
And sadness fills the air,
Where creep a hundred hairy things,
I think that I'll go there.

Where green leaves lie upon the lakes,
And gentle mists descend,
Where noises that the hedgehog makes
Seem only to offend;
Where darkness hangs above the fields,
And moles are made to roam,
Where stands the sett the badger builds,
That's where I'll call my home.

The Melancholy Cannibal

Roly-poly Herbert Hannibal
Met a melancholy cannibal.
Said the cannibal: 'Nice to meet you,
But I'm afraid I *cannot* eat you.'
And then he added, somewhat flustered,
'You see, I've just run out of custard!'

Anyone for Dennis?

One needs finesse to play tennis,
But Dennis seems to lack it.
He's much too tall to spot the ball,
And with his racket whack it.

Jingle-Jangle-Jent

A Viking liking hiking
    walked
From Katmandu to Kent,
And Timbuctu and
    Teddington
Were towns he did frequent,
And yet with everything
    he saw
And everywhere he went,
He never ever saw the sight
Of Jingle-Jangle-Jent;
He *never* ever saw the sight
Of Jingle-Jangle-Jent.

A Druid fond of fluid drank
More than you've ever
    dreamt,
It took one hundred pints
    of beer
Until he was content,
And yet with all the liquid
    that
He to his stomach sent,
He never ever knew the
    taste
Of Jingle-Jangle-Jent;
He *never* ever knew the taste
Of Jingle-Jangle-Jent.

A vet who let his pet get
    wet
In Ancient Egypt spent
His life with sickly squawks
    and squeals,
To which his ears he lent.
He learned what every
    whimper was,
What every mumble meant,
And yet he never heard the
    noise
Of Jingle-Jangle-Jent;
He *never* ever heard the noise
Of Jingle-Jangle-Jent.

A Roman roamin' round in
    Rome
Aromas did invent,
By mixing potions in a
    pot,
As over it he bent.
His nostrils were of noble
    nose,
Yet it is evident,
He never ever caught the
    whiff
Of Jingle-Jangle-Jent;
He *never* ever caught
    the whiff
Of Jingle-Jangle-Jent.

Don't Ask Me About Myself

Don't ask me about myself,
Or why I talk in stanzas,
For all the questions that you ask,
I haven't got the answers.

I may know why the world is flat,
Or why the sea is sand,
But elbow grease and trouser crease,
I cannot understand.

So ask me of freshwater fish,
And famous ballet dancers,
But don't ask me about myself,
I haven't got the answers.

The Third Bird

I taught my parrot Percival
To speak in pidgin English;
I taught him parrot-fashion,
And now he's quite a linguist.

Alas, my pigeon Peregrine
Experienced deep anguish,
At just the thought of Percival
Pronouncing pidgin language.

And so I introduced them to
My toucan, namely Terence,
For he can settle arguments
As fast as any parents.

Now they both live in harmony,
I'm sure I don't know who can
Dispute the simple theory that
One cannot do what toucan.

I've Lost my Car!

'I've lost my car, I've lost my car,
It's nowhere to be seen!
I've lost my car, I've lost my car,
And it was red and green!'

'I've found your car, I've found your car,
Outside the barber's shop!
I've found your car, I've found your car,
I am a clever cop!'

'A clever cop? Don't make me laugh,
You've no brains in your head!
The car I lost was red and green,
That car is green and red!'

Cuthbert Crow and Constance

Cuthbert Crow and Constance
Lived in a conker tree,
Whose branches stretched to heaven
With the utmost dignity.

Constance Crow was house proud,
And though the tree was big,
She dusted every single leaf
And polished every twig.

Cuthbert Crow was lazy,
He'd sit inside the nest
And wonder why the sinking sun
Should always choose the west.

When Cuthbert Crow and Constance
Went off on holiday,
Cuthbert rode upon the back
Of Constance all the way.

Tomorrow I've Given Up Hope

I've sailed all the seas in a bathtub,
And climbed all the mountains with rope,
I've flown in the skies
With soap in my eyes,
But tomorrow I've given up hope.

I've picked all the world's rarest flowers,
And seen the uncommonest trees,
I've paddled in ponds,
And made friends with fronds,
But tomorrow still quite eludes me.

I never have *seen* a tomorrow,
I've never been able to say:
'Tomorrow has come,
The bumble bees hum,
Tomorrow's come early today!'

Charlie's Cherry Tree

Every summer Charlie waited
By his Cherry Tree;
Cherries grew and Charlie picked them,
Had them for his tea.

When one summer Charlie waited,
Cherries didn't grow;
Charlie waited for a long time,
Cherries didn't show.

All through summer Charlie waited,
Autumn, winter, spring;
Charlie waited for a whole year,
Didn't get a thing.

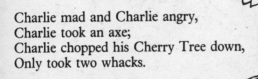

Charlie mad and Charlie angry,
Charlie took an axe;
Charlie chopped his Cherry Tree down,
Only took two whacks.

With the wood then Charlie chiselled,
Charlie made a chair;
Now he sits and Charlie wonders
What he's doing there.

Charlie sad and Charlie sorry,
Charlie wishes he
Hadn't been so hasty chopping
Down his Cherry Tree.

He Won't Say Where It Went

Famous French philosophers,
And Swiss psychiatrists,
And Austrian astrologers
Still don't know where it is.

(They've searched it with a sextant,
And they've searched it with a net;
They've searched it by the sun and moon,
And haven't seen it yet.)

But a versatile ventriloquist
Cum-conjurer from Kent
Has seen it, oh so many times,
But won't say where it went.

He won't say if it went alone,
Or if its eyes were blue,
He won't say if it sank or swam,
He won't say if it flew.

He won't say if it made a noise,
Or if it had a beard,
The only thing he'll say at all
Is that it disappeared.

A Bus Conductor
from Birmingham

A bus conductor from Birmingham
Who always says his prayers,
Prayed one day that he some day
Might be a millionaire.
(He'd travel everywhere by bus
And sit upon the stairs,
And carry nothing smaller than
A fiver for his fare.)

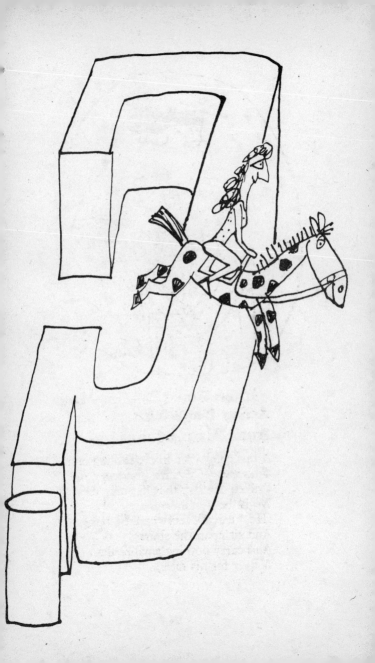

Other Books Which May be to Your Taste:

Another book that's full of fun
For folk from eight to eighty-one
Is Colin West's anthology
The Land of Utter Nonsense. He
Has also written (by himself)
A further volume for your shelf,
Entitled, unmysteriously,
Not to be Taken Seriously.